THE MOON
OF THE CHICKAREES

The Moon of the Chickarees

JEAN CRAIGHEAD GEORGE

Illustrated by JOHN SCHOENHERR

Thomas Y. Crowell Company   New York

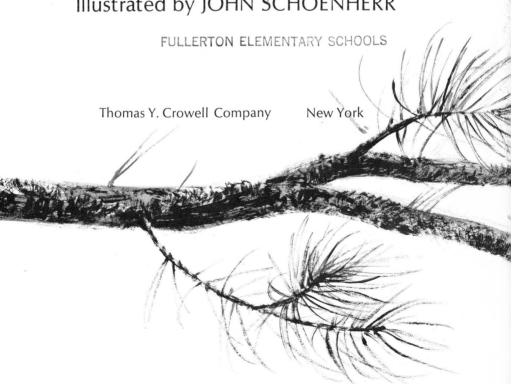

599
Geo
c-6

MANUFACTURED IN THE UNITED STATES OF AMERICA

L.C. Card 68-11064

1   2   3   4   5   6   7   8   9   10

By the Author

The sun arose. The sky turned yellow. The faintest hint of green showed on the April land. A furry face appeared in the hollow of a lodgepole pine. *"TCHER-r-r-r-r-r-rrrrr, TECHERRRR-r-r-r-r-r-r!"* The screamer's breath turned to ice stars in the cold air.

She was a red squirrel, about eleven inches long, and rusty red. From the tops of the hardwood forests of New England, the lodgepoles and firs of the West, and the pines of the Southwest, the red squirrels spend hours each day announcing the presence of animals around them, whether they be bears, jays, magpies, woodpeckers, gray squirrels, house cats—an endless list—skunks, lynxes, martens, and, in the loudest voice of all, other red squirrels. They are the "boomers" of the South and East, the "bummers" on the Pacific Coast, and the "Douglas chickarees" of the Rocky Mountains.

"*TCHERrrrrrrrrrrr,*" the chickaree in the hole rasped at a gray Canada jay. He was accustomed to her noise for he had shared the same pines all winter. He answered her scolding with a mere flick of his wings as he flew off to chase a newly emerged beetle. The chickaree washed her face, brushed her ears, then looked down the fourteen feet onto her small domain in the forest. It was only seventy feet across and sixty feet in length.

3

Her land lay along the Bitterroot River in Montana. Above it, streams, full with melted snow from the Clearwater Mountains on the west and the Sapphire Mountains on the east, ran deep and cold that April morning. They sprinted through forests of pine and fir, cascaded past mountain meadows, leaped around rock slides, then rolled into the Bitterroot River. One rivulet splashed in its rock bed not far from the chickaree's tree. She could see it spring through her pines and hear it tinkle into her river thicket of willows and aspens, flowers and grasses.

4

The crescent moon rose soon after the sun, but the chickaree did not see it, for it was below the dark peaks of the Clearwater Mountains. Furthermore, she was watching her cousin, an adventurous chickaree who lived beyond the granite boulder.

He was sneaking through the tender cow parsnips toward her store of toadstools and mushrooms. She had dried them last autumn and hidden them under the bark of a limb on an old western hemlock. This had taken her weeks.

Now they were about to be packed into her

cousin's cheeks, and she could do nothing about it. She had just given birth to four babies, naked and hairless, and she could not leave them in the cold to chase her cousin.

"*TSCHIC KERrrrrr!*" she exploded as he sat down and took a mushroom in his front paws. So earsplitting was her order that she disturbed the magpie in the river thicket. The magpie, a splendid black and white bird with a long wedge-shaped tail, had returned to the Bitterroot three weeks before after a winter of wandering east to Wisconsin. A member of the crow family, he was almost as expressive as the chickaree.

He "yakked" back at her, then stabbed one of the opening buds on the narrowleaf cottonwood under his feet. The tree was pale green with the first leaves of the April moon.

The chickaree did not hear the magpie. She was too angry. Once more she scolded her cousin, this time so fiercely that he jumped to the limb that led over the boulder. Flicking his elegant brush of a tail, he ran home.

The chickaree pulled her babies into her belly fur and held them against the cold. The frost that

6

tingled outside the hollow had whitened the sprouting blades of winter grain as far south as Kansas and had nipped the cherry blossoms in Michigan.

The chickaree knew nothing of these things.

As the hours passed and the day warmed to April's glowing 40° F. temperature, she felt only the sucking of her young. Their eyes were closed and their tails and legs were so short that they did not even vaguely resemble their acrobatic father. The chickaree had mated with him on an early March dawn in the falling snow. Now, forty days later, on this April day, she was tending his babies, just as her mother had tended her a year ago. The chickaree did not remember her mother's tongue or her hugging legs and paws. She did not remember being rolled on her back, tipped on her side, and bitten lovingly. She cared for her own children out of unconscious memories and an inherited code of red squirrel behavior.

Like her own babies were doing now, the chickaree had nursed and slept. After ten days velvet fur

fuzzed over her body. In twenty-seven days her eyes and ears opened. She was weaned in five weeks. Then she and her brothers and sisters ventured out of the den. They practiced zipping from limb to limb, their tails extended, their legs spread wide. Grasping tiny twigs, they bounced and swung in the speckled shade. They ran in whispering rain, and they followed their mother to her three-foot-high storehouses of pine seeds and berries on the ground.

Last August the chickaree left home. She crept gingerly through the forest trees, moving and hesitating, running and hiding. Other chickarees shrieked at her when she stepped on their land or ran past their storehouses. When they did, she rippled her tail and hurried on down the valley of the Bitterroot.

One morning she climbed the big lodgepole pine. No red squirrels challenged her, for at last she had found a small patch of land that no chickaree claimed as its own.

She made this her home and learned every limb, twig, and knothole on it, as she collected seeds, cones and berries, mushrooms and fruits. With the ripening of cones and nuts in the autumn the chickaree was busy. All day she cut them from the trees, dropped them to the ground, then collected them into three- and four-foot-high piles. Some of these things she preserved. Green pine and fir cones she placed in a quiet pool so they would not dry out and drop their seeds. Mushrooms and toadstools she laid in the sun to dry. She buried berries in needles in her storehouses to keep them fresh.

And while she worked she scolded and screamed. She fussed at the jays, the pack rats, the mice, the woodpeckers, and the nuthatches, for her food stores tempted them all.

In November she met her cousin for the first time. Her back was turned, but she saw him out of the corners of her eyes. He was sneaking over the boulder toward one of her storehouses. She flipped herself around, flashed her tail, and, exploding in wrath, scared him back to his own land.

When the winds howled cold and the leaves blew off the willows and basswoods the chickaree built herself a winter nest in the crotch of a western hemlock. She made it both windproof and rainproof with leaves, pine needles, moss, and dry twigs. It was about twenty inches wide and a foot deep. She lined the center of the room with rootlets and soft fibers. Here she lived all winter as the moons came and went, bringing the season of the snowfalls and snowdrifts that locked up the hills of the Bitterroot.

And then April entered. White starflowers came up and opened. Balsamroot grew toward the sun and flowered with fragrance. The birds sang again, the fish swirled after miller moths, and the chickaree left her winter home and moved to the old woodpecker's hole in the pine. There she had her babies, licking each one's nose to help him breathe.

Across the river on the flats, the sage grouse assembled to perform their dance of courtship. They came through blooming sage and buttercups to gather on their dancing stage, a circle they had cleared in the chaparral.

Three males strutted, heads back, white chests shining below black throats. Spreading their spiked tail feathers to display every gleaming inch, they

beat their feet, flicked their wings, and jumped. Females gathered nearby and seemed to ignore the males, even when they puffed their yellow air sacs and boomed. When the dance was done they all walked off to eat. This was only the first of their dancing days, and the ceremony was short. Each day it would be longer, until all were mated.

The chickaree did not hear the sage grouse boom. She was rolling her babies with her tongue, helping to stimulate the action of their lungs and their bloodstreams. Finally, when they were dry and quiet, she peered out her door and looked at April along the Bitterroot. Holly grapes bloomed in the sunshine and the golden flowers of the glacier lilies nodded in the wind. The chickaree turned her head and glanced up at the mountain. Beyond her gaze, the young bald eagles were breaking out of their shells. They struggled and rested their heavy heads on the great platform of sticks in the wind-torn fir.

The chickaree closed her eyes and listened to the forest. The magpie called to his mate; he held a stick in his beak. His mate lifted her feathers in approval and he carried it to the basswood. He jammed it in a wide crotch, and it became the first of many that would be stacked into a nest. He stepped back and looked at it. *"MAAAG,"* he cried. The chickaree heard his comment.

Suddenly she drew back in surprise. *"TCHErr!"* A tree swallow hovered at her door. Just back from the Gulf Coast, the bird was nest-hunting, peeking into every hole in the forest to see if it was suitable. He wheeled away at the squirrel's announcement of occupancy.

17

The chickaree heard something stirring in the dry leaves, and she looked out to see who was digging. Below, the flowers and leaves of a biscuitroot trembled as a field mouse dug at its roots. The chickaree only clucked, a soft sound that said "I know you are there." She did not scold, for he was no threat. He was not after her stores.

As the chickaree babies grew, the mother did not need to lick and feed them so often. She spent more time watching the woods for creatures. One morning she left early and went headfirst down her tree, listening to the *KILLIE KILLIE* of the sparrowhawk. Only a week ago this small, colorful falcon had returned from his wintering grounds in the south.

At first he had sat quietly in the stubs, catching insects and mice in the sagebrush. Now he was reclaiming his old home across the Bitterroot, announcing his boundaries and driving his neighbors beyond them. His nest would not be ready for another two weeks; his young would not hatch until June.

Higher up the mountain an early nester, the redtailed hawk, had eggs. Every three hours the female stood up on her stick nest and carefully turned the eggs with her beak to keep the embryos from sticking to the shells. Then she spread her feathers, sat down, and relaxed into the broody silence of incubation, while the snowdrops and blue-eyed Marys bobbed in the wind below her.

Other life was beginning. High up the mountain among the rocks and balsamroot, the bighorn sheep were lambing. The mothers-to-be lay waiting in rocky caves. The ewes and the young lambs of a year ago grazed together. The rams, in their own groups, followed the receding snow up-mountain, nosing the flowers of the golden weeds and chewing the greening grasses.

One night as the three-quarter moon rose over the valley of the Bitterroot River, the mother chickaree lay beside her babies. They were now too

big for her to tuck them in her warm belly fur and curl over them as she had done before.

When the sun came up the babies awoke and nursed. The chickaree looked out her door. A coyote was ambling along the river edge. She screamed. Her cousin heard her and he also screamed. Another chickaree answered them both. Another April morning had started. The mother went to her door. With a flick of her tail she jumped from her hollow to the limb below. Quietly she ran to the ground.

She did not stop until she reached the pine cones
she had stored in the water. She peeled off the
sheaths, ate the seeds, then loped to her berry
cache. She swallowed some of these hastily and
skittered up a pine tree to run her limb route to
the river thicket. This took her to the cottonwood
where the magpies were building their nest. They
dived at her, for occasionally chickarees rob magpies' eggs and nestlings. The chickaree fled. A
hole in her ear marked the spot where a female
magpie had struck her last summer. The angry
birds came on.

The chickaree circled a pine stub and plunged into a hole on its far side. Unfortunately it was occupied by the redheaded woodpecker that had lived in the forest all year with the chickaree. He was chipping a nest cavity. The woodpecker slashed at the chickaree. She clutched a small limb with her front claws, trapezed to a bigger one, flipped to a tree trunk, and crawled under a piece of hanging bark. The woodpecker and magpies flew by.

One noon the chickaree ran to the river thicket to collect the greening aspen buds. She took a route she knew well, up trunks and down limbs. Suddenly, the trail ended in space. A tree was missing. It had been cut down during the night by the beaver and now lay near his den in the riverbank. Its bark would be eaten by his mate who was sleeping with her four newborn kits.

The chickaree was vaguely annoyed that her roadway had been interrupted, but she quickly recovered, scolded, jumped to a buckthorn, and spiraled to the ground. Instantly she remembered having been in this spot before. She dug furiously until she found a hazelnut she had buried in a grass hummock.

The hazelnut was no longer tasty. The coming of the April moon had changed it. The seed had absorbed the melted snow and its respiration had increased. As it breathed—in the manner of a plant—its metabolism began to rise and chemical changes took place. New minerals formed. They moved to the embryo and the embryo sent down a root. The chickaree did not find the germinating nut palatable. She left it in the soil, where it would become a tree.

Suddenly she heard the rattle of pine cones. Someone was in her storehouse! She rushed through the aspen limbs, balancing herself with her tail, and leaped to the forest floor. *"TCHERR-r-r-r-rrrrrrrr."* A pack rat, foraging deep among the shelled cones, held still at her cry.

The chickaree dove angrily into one of the tunnels in her pile, searching for the rat. Bursting out through a wall, he ran forty yards to his own castle of treasures. He slipped into his pile of grass and seeds and lay still beside his most cherished possessions—a bottletop, a fish hook, and one shiny dime he had found by the river.

The chickaree scolded and scolded while the mother pack rat and her fifteen-day-old young stared out of their home in the rocks nearby.

The chickaree ran over the ground until she came to her biggest storehouse, a three-foot-high and four-foot-long gathering of cones and nut shells. A thieving chickadee flew away from it when she arrived, but the first young mice of the year stayed, scrambling in and out of the tunnels they had made in her stores. She screamed: It was time to feed her babies but she could not. She *had* to defend her storehouses. In great conflict, she

26

ground her teeth for three full minutes. Then she sat still and listened. The forest was silent. Contentedly she climbed to her family. Halfway up the pine she saw the magpie alight on her toadstool supply on the hemlock limb. *"THERRRRR,"* she cried. She was about to charge the bird when she heard her hungry babies screech. The sound pulled her up the tree as if she were on a string. She flipped her fuzzy tail and slipped into the hollow. No sooner had she fed and washed them than the April happenings called her away again.

The magpie was nervous. She was in the water taking her afternoon bath, but she watched the sky constantly. Lifting her wings, dipping her head, she would stop bathing and stoop as if to fly. Suddenly the magpie cried a soft alarm to her mate, ran ashore, and slipped under a log.

The chickaree had learned that the birds, with their keen eyesight, saw enemies long before she did. When the magpie hid, the chickaree hid in a knothole and then looked about. A red-tailed hawk

dropped into view, his wings motionless as he rode the lifting winds above the river. The chickaree watched the hawk, for he would kill her if he could. Well hidden, she warned the forest of his presence. *"KKK, kk-kkkk!"* Every bird stopped what he was doing at this note and quietly moved out of sight. *"KKKKRrr!"* This cry was so piercing it awakened the pine marten who had been sleeping at the top of a pine.

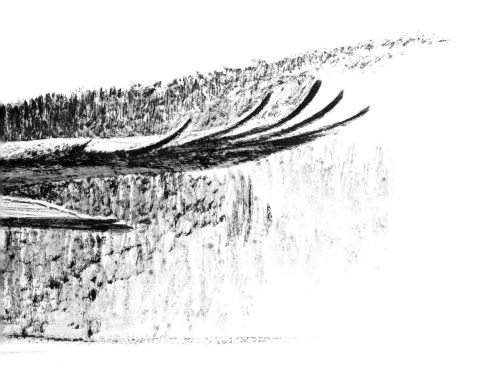

The marten was a tree-climbing relative of the mink and the weasel. Dark and slender, he moved with the grace of flowing water and the speed of lightning. Chickarees were his favorite food. He listened to the mother's voice, swaying his long graceful neck as he tried to locate her. He could not. Rippling almost imperceptibly he flowed to a lower limb.

The woodpecker, flying to an insect-riddled tree, saw the pine marten move. *"YK,"* he warned and

clung to the back of a tree where the marten could not see him. The chickaree heard his sharp warning cry and sensed "pine marten." She stayed in the knothole. She waited.

A bird sang. *"PILL-will-will."* The willet was in the river thicket. He had dropped onto a clump of grass to stare at it. The willet nested in the grasses along the shore and, during the moon of April, he too hunted for the perfect nesting site. He investigated every tall clump of grass. This one inspired him to walk into it and cock an eye.

Suddenly he saw the marten flow down the limb.
Calling a warning to his mate he sat down and held
still. His colors blended with the brown grass.

The tree swallows heard the warning call of the
willet. They spread out over the river. *"CHI-veet,"*
they called as they passed along the sound of
danger.

The marten stood up. The birds and the chick-aree had disappeared. He yawned, and his pointed nose wrinkled. Gathering his powerful legs under him, he leaped twenty feet to the next tree and ran down the limbs deep into the forest. He would sleep until dark and then set out again. He had five young in a hollow tree, but he never went near them, for the male marten is solitary after mating in July.

The chickaree still did not move. Presently a song sparrow bubbled his "all's well" song and the red squirrel knew the marten had departed. She skittered to the top of her storehouse and began chattering.

That afternoon, after a midday quiet period, the chickaree listened to the male birds that arrived early and began their nesting rites in April. They sat boldly in the open, on the tips of tree limbs, as they sang to establish property rights and to call mates to their land. Because they were exposed, some would be killed by hawks. The April moon is a dangerous time for them.

Down by the river a brown and white song sparrow sang a warning song. The bird had returned from the South to find that a strange male had arrived earlier than he and had taken his nesting grounds. If his own mate came back she would accept the stranger as her partner, for the females returned to the property, not to a particular male. The song sparrow wanted his land and his mate.

He flew to a willow twig and faced his opponent. Then he lifted his feathers until he was as round as a ball. The raised feathers were frightening to the strange male, but he did not fly. The song sparrow lifted his wings and vibrated them. Terrified by this the invader hid under a young budding cottonwood.

The song sparrow continued harassing him. Still puffed, singing a low song, he flew at the other male—the threat dance of the song sparrow.

The invader could face him no longer. He whirled around, flew to the bend in the river, and sped out of the territory.

When he was gone the song sparrow closed his feathers, threw back his head, and burst into his song of ownership.

The chickaree heard and stopped chattering briefly. That moment the needs of her young pulled her back to the pine. She climbed swiftly, looked across her domain, and screamed. Her cousin was back. She ran down the tree and chased him so far she found herself in his property—on a stone in a sunny rockslide.

Suddenly terror filled her. In a crevice not two feet away lay a rattlesnake, its heart-shaped head swinging slowly on its arched neck. The snake had just come out of its hibernating state and was bathing in the sunlight. He moved slowly; he was still too cold to be quick. The chickaree sensed this and her courage returned. Leaping up four feet, she grabbed a tree twig that bounced dangerously low, then slowly rode upward where she grabbed a bigger limb and was safe. She hurried back to her babies. Her fear passed slowly. The little chickarees felt it and circled closely around her, sensing for the first time that the world beyond their hollow was dangerous.

While the chickaree fed her young, a gray and white Canada jay came to the river thicket. He cocked his head. Into the warm sun crept newly hatched caterpillars. They buckled and humped as they climbed twigs and grass blades. Millions had hatched along the Bitterroot during the time of the April moon. Their emergence was timed to the greening of the plants just as the birds' return from the South was timed to the awakening of the insect hordes. The jay stabbed at a caterpillar. As he did, it reared its head and tail and curled into a circle. Now it looked so much like a bud that the bird did not recognize it as food. He ignored it and hopped to another twig.

Other insects were emerging. Out of the water burst a few black flies, the first of the year. All winter they had clung to submerged rocks. They were in their larval stage and looked like little palm trees, the "leaves" of which paddled food into their mouths. Today the palm trees began to split, and as they did the adult flies stepped from the cases and floated to the surface in a bubble of air. They spread their wings, and soared upward. The tree swallows dived and shot after them, sweeping many into their mouths.

39

The chickaree came out of her hollow to see the jay on her cone pile, throwing back hulls and gobbling seeds.

This was the last robbery she could bear!

Chattering continuously, she raced to her winter home. It was close by her storehouses and easier to look out of than the deep, protected hollow where she had given birth. She went into the leafy nest, nosed back the lining, repaired a few holes, and rushed back to her hollow. Picking up a furry baby by her teeth, she carried it down the trunk, over the ground, up the winter nest tree, and placed it inside. She went back for another.

When all were gathered, the mother chickaree lay down, her head out her doorway. At last she was content. She was near her storehouses and yet still with her babies. She began to talk to the forest, clucking and chattering her teeth until the sun went down and the fading moon of April passed high overhead.

ABOUT THE AUTHOR

The enthusiastic reception that young people accord each new book by Jean Craighead George is warmly seconded by their parents, teachers, and librarians. Mrs. George is coauthor of *Dipper of Copper Creek,* which received the Aurianne Award for the most outstanding animal story published in 1957. *My Side of the Mountain, The Summer of the Falcon, Gull Number 737, Spring Comes to the Ocean, Coyote in Manhattan,* and each of the books in The Thirteen Moons series have affirmed her remarkable sensitivity both to the world of nature and to young people.

Mrs. George is a regular contributor of nature stories to *Reader's Digest.* She has held the position of art editor for *Pageant* magazine and has served as a newspaper reporter for the *Washington Post* and International News Service.

ABOUT THE ARTIST

John Schoenherr was graduated from Pratt Institute with a B.F.A. degree and also studied at the Art Students League of New York. Mr. Schoenherr illustrates articles and stories for *Reader's Digest* and *Analog: Science Fiction and Science Fact.* A recipient of four Citations of Merit from the Society of Illustrators, he also received the Hugo Award in 1965 as the Best Science Fiction Artist of that year. Mr. Schoenherr, who has traveled to Europe, the Caribbean, and the western United States, now makes his home in Stockton, New Jersey, with his family.